What's Your
Impact on Business

The Sherpa Guide to
Business, Behavior and You

D0067851

Other Books by
Brenda Corbett and/or Rubi Ho

The Sherpa Guide: Process-Driven Executive Coaching

BE ... don't do: The Sherpa Guide to Coaching for Managers

The Sherpa Guide to Who You Are

More Than a Game

Confronting My Elephants

WHAT'S YOUR

IMPACT ON

BUSINESS

THE SHERPA GUIDE TO BUSINESS, BEHAVIOR AND YOU

BRENDA CORBETT & RUBI HO

'Impact on Business' is replacing 'Return on Investment' as a measure of the value of leadership development. Seven years of research proves the need for a new standard. Impact on Business is it. IOB.

Learn about IOB as you enjoy seven stories about people you probably work with: classic cases that show the importance of business behavior for the bottom line.

As you read through the stories in this book I am sure that your first reaction will be: "I am not like any of these people." The truth is that everyone displays some degree of this behavior at some time in their professional career. That is why the lessons in this book are so important to each and every one of us. Take your time as you read through these stories, then examine yourself very closely while keeping an eye on your business behavior throughout each and every day.

Andy Hove
Chief Operating Officer
Mistral Group
Bethesda, Maryland, USA

With Rubi Ho's executive leadership expertise and guidance, everyone here at Orr Corporation is making significant strides in their leadership behavior, resulting in a positive impact on business for our company. The bottom line is this: behavior matters just as much as business results. Both are integral for a company's overall success. The leadership experts at Sherpa Coaching exemplify this model by their focus on Impact on Business.

Ray Aldridge
Chief Executive Officer
Orr Corporation
Louisville, Kentucky, USA

Just as Sherpa guides lead climbers in ascending a mountain, Brenda Corbett and Rubi Ho lead us on a smoother path to success in our professional lives. I would take these authors on my climb of Kilimanjaro, or have them lead me to the top of Everest any day.

Marshall Goldsmith
Executive Coach
Best-selling author
Rancho Santa Fe, California, USA

Published 2012 by Sherpa Coaching, Cincinnati, Ohio USA

The characters described in our stories are real. Their names, personal information and the details of their operating environments have been changed to respect their confidentiality.

This book contains principles from executive education programs offered by the authors at the University of Georgia, Texas Christian and Miami University.

Executive education programs can be arranged directly with the authors for on-site delivery, as they have done for Toyota, the National Cancer Institute, Duke Energy and many others.

Cover art and layout by Ian McAfee and Mike Leporati
Printing by Pocket-Pak, The Colony, TX, USA
Distributed by Sasha Corporation, Cincinnati, Ohio, USA
Preproduction consultant: Diane Dew

Single copy and bulk purchases of this book can be made at the authors' online store, at www.sherpacoaching.com/store. Quantity discounts apply.

For more information about Sherpa Coaching's services and products, contact:

Sherpa Coaching
(513) 232-0002
PO Box 417240
Cincinnati, Ohio, USA 45241
info@sherpacoaching.com
www.sherpacoaching.com

This book is dedicated to YOU

This book brings you seven stories, each one as real, as raw, and as true as they come. You might even find yourself in here somewhere.

This book is the beginning of a journey. It's not meant to solve your problems; it's meant to show the dramatic impact you can have in this world, in your work environment, and everywhere else in life.

Table of Contents

Foreword

The benefits of coaching at any level are well documented. Many of the world's top performers benefit from coaching, whether in sports, performing arts or business. What leads the very best to actively seek further coaching support? The answer is clear: the best in their professions achieve enormous success through a combination of technical or functional expertise and an in-depth understanding of how to lead others.

This book highlights that special combination of skill and behavior, the two primary elements in the equation for success. Combined, skills and behavior create an "Impact on Business," or IOB. In the world of high performing business organizations, Impact on Business serves as the strategic value proposition for executive coaching. The authors of this book address the concept of IOB through a combination of thought-evoking vignettes and the power of "Sherpa questions."

On a personal level, my introduction to coaching came in 2009, as a participant in the Sherpa executive coaching certification program. What began as an interesting framework for self-awareness quickly became a comprehensive playbook for coaches who help others realize their full potential, reaching their "personal summit."

As a student, coaching client, and executive sponsor, I have seen first-hand the tremendous impact of the Sherpa process. It affects clients both personally and professionally and often leads to a groundswell of interest for further coaching support in an organization. The success of coaching is not limited to personal growth. It also provides the foundation for broader success within a client's team or organization.

Great coaching can have a profound impact on business. Leaders progress through varying levels in an organization, initially because of their ability to deliver results or functional expertise. For leaders to achieve even greater success, their focus must shift from their specific expertise or ability toward helping others achieve the same results. This is where the second half of the IOB equation, behavior, becomes so critical to success. Without focus on both skills and leadership behavior, leaders are not likely to realize their full potential as their success becomes increasingly dependent on their team's performance.

As you read this book, I challenge you to compare and contrast the leaders in our seven stories. Where are the similarities? Where are the differences? What are you learning from their experiences? If you see yourself, I encourage you to seek out feedback, formally and informally. Embrace the feedback. Don't defend against it. Soon, you will begin to realize the true benefits of awareness and a renewed commitment to growth.

In closing and on a more personal level, I would like to thank Brenda Corbett and the entire Sherpa team, who have worked tirelessly in supporting and developing leaders around the world. They are making a difference, one client at a time. They have been instrumental in my development and in changing the way in which development professionals affect the business. It is a privilege to share my perspective on IOB and, more broadly, Sherpa Coaching.

Stephen Subasic
Vice President, Human Resources
Stanley Black & Decker, Inc.
April 2012

Success and Happiness

At the end of the day, you want to be fulfilled. You want to be complete. You want to have it all. The 'total package' means being happy and successful. So, let's talk about happiness and success.

What is success? You are successful when you set meaningful goals and reach them. Unfortunately, you don't always achieve this. You work for a living, yet cannot find any meaning or satisfaction in your labor.

What is happiness? Go a step further; what is complete happiness? Break it down: complete happiness means being happy and being complete. You are completely happy when your relationships with people are positive and productive. Happiness, all on its own, can be found in a number of seductive sources.

Complete happiness requires a complete person.

Can you say that you are complete?

How do you become completely happy? Completion of self is a relatively new concept in the Western World. In many places, it's an ancient concept, especially in the Far East. We went on a search to discover how to be completely happy. In the process, we worked with Arun Kattel, a sociologist in Kathmandu, Nepal. We interviewed Sherpas who have summited Mount Everest. We asked them about success and happiness. We asked them about their work, their lives and what really matters to them.

What did we find out from the Sherpas? We expected something powerful and unique and that's what we got. Throughout this book, we will share Sherpa Inspiration: wisdom that relates to what you do every day. These Sherpas have personally stood atop the highest point on earth and have helped countless others to attain the summit. Here's what we learned: This takes work. It's no surprise, but finding 'success and happiness' takes work. Lots of work.

No matter what you do, no matter what you say, no matter how you act, everything you do that relates to 'success, happiness, and completion of self' takes work.

This takes work, but you work all the time. We challenge you to ask: are you working on yourself? Frankly, working on yourself has become a lost art. Our mission is to bring that work ethic back. The lost part of our being is an ethic that says: "I am going to work on myself." This involves thinking differently. This involves reflecting differently. This involves speaking differently and acting differently. Ultimately, this involves brand new behavior.

Once you know how to work on your 'self,' you will be rewarded. You will discover that all the work is worth it. We know this truth: people who change their behavior for the better become better people. They gain success and happiness.

Without any additional effort, they also improve everything around them: their relationships and the organizations they serve.

People who work on their behavior will ultimately make different choices. They will be successful. They will choose to be happy.

As you read this book, you'll discover how important you are and how much influence you really have.

You have an impact on your business, your relationships, and a lot more.

Read on, and learn how to make the most of that impact.

The Business of Life

Let's face it; much of your happiness will be tied up in your work. You spend so many hours there. If there is one place you should focus on improving your happiness, it's at work. If you are good at what you do, you can be successful. Shouldn't you be happy, too? When you work for a living with all of your heart, you have power and influence. Your power and influence can make your organization and its people happier and more successful. Most importantly, this can make you happier and more successful. We call that having a "positive impact on business."

At the end of the day, it's figuring out how to channel all you are into what you do. If you want to be good at your job, you have to know what you are doing. Your knowledge and skill help create your Impact on Business. But, IOB is more than knowledge and skill. Your Impact on Business is directly related to your behavior. When you display positive business behavior, the rest of your life will get better too.

What is IOB?

Simply put, IOB stands for Impact on Business. When you deliver a positive Impact on Business, you are producing a significant improvement in the way things turn out for your organization. If you want to be happy and successful, then delivering a positive Impact on Business should be your ultimate goal. This formula tells you how to deliver the biggest impact, right where you are.

I.O.B.
Positive Skills + Positive Behavior = Positive Impact on Business ™

Positive Skills:

Leave skills out of the equation and performance will eventually fall short. For example: take an expert well versed in her field; she is the vice president of IT in a large hospital. Here are some of the skills she must have to be competent in her job.

Skills:
- Regulating Medical Records
- Financial Management
- Cost Analysis
- Forecasting
- Network Tuning

Positive Behavior:

Let's look at the other half of the equation. Our vice president has five people reporting directly to her, with another 33 people reporting to them. To lead, guide and motivate them. She will need certain positive behaviors.

Behaviors:
- Leadership
- Communication
- Problem Solving
- Follow Through
- Approachability

She knows all the 'ins and outs' of her profession. She needs certain positive behaviors in order to lead effectively.

True success comes from a combination of positive skills and positive behavior. Together, the two create a positive Impact on Business.

What happens to a person with great style and charisma, who lacks essential knowledge and experience?

What about someone who has great technical skills and no personality?

Either one will be a disaster. Both skills and behavior must be positive in order to create a positive Impact on Business.

Sherpa Inspiration: Are You Ready?

The way you behave and treat others is a personal choice. Perhaps you are ready to embrace this truth. Maybe you're not. You are responsible for that choice. You have the power, but it takes work.

In the back of your mind, you are asking:

➜ "Why should I have to change?

➜ "What about them? They are the ones who are incompetent, not me.

➜ "They can't handle themselves in a meeting. They don't get the job done. They should change."

We get it. We know. We have seen them and we have coached them. You're right; they should change. At the end of the day, however, you can only change yourself. We don't care about those other people. We only care about YOU.

This book is about you. It seems like a paradox: you have power, but can't control anyone but yourself. That's just part of the truth. You cannot directly change other peoples' behavior.

However, you can change it indirectly. When your behavior gets better, theirs will too. We guarantee it. Believe it.

In this book, you are going to read seven real life stories. As you read, we hope you discover that changes in behavior (even very small ones) will create huge impact in your life, especially in your relationships.

Better relationships help create happiness: your happiness. As you read our stories, we hope you also see part of yourself in these real people. We hope you can identify with them and the people around them.

You've been there. We'll help you sort it out, and help you develop a personal game plan to achieve success and happiness.

·

The Stories

We are going to tell you seven stories about seven people we personally worked with. These stories are all true. Here is our cast of characters:

 Sam
Chief Financial Officer at a manufacturing firm in Kansas. Cold as ice.

 Alicia
Texas call center manager. Perfect. Too perfect.

Christian
Silicon Valley. Small IT company president. He doesn't really like people.

Robert
Sales manager. Detroit, Michigan. Loves to talk . . . and talk . . . and talk.

Danielle
Deputy Commissioner, health care. She's
not approachable, but she doesn't care.

 ### Nora
District Manager, cosmetics manufacturing.
Lost in New Jersey. Nora's act is a
vanishing act.

Duane
Marketing manager in sunny Florida.
Beautiful loser. They call him
'The Doormat.'

Our challenge for you is simple: as you read, try to relate these stories to your own working life. Become aware of the way these people behave, and their Impact on Business. Be honest. Do you see your boss? Do you spot someone you know? Do you see yourself?

Look at things from every angle, from different perspectives. In each story, there's a behavior issue. Learn what it is. Then, apply the learning in whatever way makes you happy and successful.

An obligation comes to you, because you are reading this book. Here's what we expect from you:

➤ First, be open and just take in the information. Let your guard down. Read and seek to understand, not defend or justify.

➤ Second, reflect. Reflect on the story. Reflect on the individual. Reflect on yourself. Be honest. Acknowledge the truth; do you have room to grow in this area?

➤ Third, spend time with the 'Sherpa Inspiration' that we offer after every story. They are there to help you create full awareness and understanding.

➤ And lastly, be willing to play a different tune. Be willing to be more conscientious with people, with your words, with how you act and behave. Be willing to live out your Impact on Business in a more positive way.

Your positive changes will surprise you more than you know. They will surprise others. You will discover that it's worth all the effort.

Sherpa Inspiration: A Tough Climb

Let's face it; dealing with behavioral issues is very tough. We know this and do not take it lightly. We know it is hard to do this alone. Real changes in behavior take time, effort, willingness, an effective process, and a whole lot of practice and accountability.

We typically spend at least three months with our clients to create something sustainable and meaningful for them and for their organization. We are sharing the secrets our clients have learned.

The biggest secret is an attitude that creates positive changes in the way you look at yourself. That's the starting point, summed up in these few words:

➔ Start by becoming more aware.

➔ Notice things.

The second secret is an action, a change in behavior that makes things better:

➲ Plan alternative actions.

➲ Do something differently.

For us, that first critical piece is one of awareness and understanding, combined with your willingness to take one little step.

When it comes to doing something differently, just take it one step at a time. That one little step belongs to you and only you. No one can do the work for you.

Success and happiness.

If you want it, you can have it.

Sam
My Way or the Highway

Sam is the chief financial officer for an auto parts maker in Shawnee Mission, Kansas. Sam's employer is a good sized firm, and they've done their best to keep people on the payroll, in good times and bad alike. Sam has been brilliant in his strategies and tactics. He's kept costs down. He's kept up with reporting regulations. In fact, Sam has kept the company afloat.

People who work with Sam will tell you that he is very talented, but he's as cold as ice. The guy never says 'Hello' to anyone. Sam walks in from the parking lot and bolts to his office. He closes the door and opens it only if he needs to shout out his next demand: "Kerry, get in here. Mike, where's that report I need?" Everyone shudders when they hear the door open. They hope their name won't be called.

Here's how Sam describes his style:

"It's my way or the highway. Otherwise, you can take the dead end street, the U-turn . . . whatever you want to do. My way or the highway means my ideas are going to be the best. Nobody here can come up with ideas as good as mine.

"I hire people to do the work. I'll do the thinking. But, with all that, I am surrounded by incompetence. I have to tell these people what to do, or they will fail and it will be on my head. All these people have to do is what I tell them to do. That's the simple recipe for success.

"I believe in the truth. Sometimes people don't like it. Sometimes feelings get hurt. I didn't include someone. I didn't need to. Sorry. I might have even yelled at them. So? Do you think I have time to bring them into the office for a happy little conversation? I have too much to do. No time to slow down, let alone be concerned for how they feel.

"I have a job to do and I do it. People fail, and I react. What's the problem? These people just don't 'get' me. I don't care if they understand me, as long as they do the work and do it right. I do not need people asking 'What about this? What about that?' Come on people, you know I have been in this business fifteen years! I know what I am doing."

Do you know someone who manages the way Sam does? Of course you do. There are people like Sam everywhere. If he is not in your office, he's down the block.

Maybe we are talking about you here. Is that possible, to some degree? Have you ever thought, felt or acted the way Sam does? Maybe you don't do it all the time, but . . . Have you ever 'run over' somebody to get what you wanted?

If so, consider: maybe what you wanted was clearly the right thing, but you got there the wrong way.

Start embracing this truth: if this is you, you are creating a world of intimidation with yourself at the center. An environment like this makes people shut down. Eventually, all communication shuts down.

Management by intimidation is one of the most prevalent behaviors that executive coaches deal with. What's the Impact on Business created by intimidation? Think about working for Sam.

How do you feel? It's called lack of empowerment.

When you dominate instead of cooperate, you do not empower your people. If you don't empower people, they never learn to do anything on their own. If you leave, who will replace you? Ultimately, you will be a leader with no followers.

Intimidation can change into something better if you become available and open to your people.

Here's where a new attitude can make a difference. If you are intimidating, acknowledge it. Understand and own it: this might be you. You will not be able to move forward unless you own the fact that you behave this way. Here's the great part: If you can identify that you behave this way, you can change it.

Just as you want your family to succeed, you want your company to succeed. You want it to work like a fine, well-oiled machine. If you can step back and see the damage you are doing, things will start to change on their own. Your task is simple. Be aware and see what's going on. Understand the implications and you will start traveling down a different path, a more positive one.

Sherpa Inspiration: Be Available

We live inside people's business lives. We observe. We coach. As we share our stories, we will highlight certain behaviors and call them what they are.

We'll help you understand the cost of your current behaviors, how they affect your life at work and everything else you do.

As coaches, we simply act as a conduit, a pipeline which delivers a new way of understanding yourself.

Think of your current habits as a tennis game: The ball comes over the net and you hit it back, the same way every time. You're not winning points. What do you do? You have to do something different if you're going to be successful.

Maybe you'll hit the ball diagonally cross court, creating a fresh new angle that gets you beyond the routine, and past your opponent. Perhaps you'll go over the top, throw up a lob, put the ball in a high arc into the back of the court for a winner.

Whatever you do, you have to play the game differently.
Be available to look at your situation with a twist. You can change the circumstances in front of you. You just have to be open and accessible to the idea of not handling a scenario like you always have.

Until you behave differently, you won't be as happy as you should be, and you won't be as successful.

So what does your cross court shot look like? How about your lob?

Let's look at our next story.

Alicia
Perfect, Almost Perfect

Meet Alicia. Take a look at her office in this Beaumont call center, and you'll have to admit: Alicia's office is immaculate, spotless. Things look as if they are glued to the desk. It's that perfect. If you move something, she takes it from your hand and puts it right back in its place.

Alicia recently took four months to complete an important project that could have been done in half the time. She had her reasons: she was assigned to a new office; her assistant went on maternity leave; her favorite lunch items in the cafeteria were taken off the menu. You could say Alicia doesn't handle changes very well.

Let's hear what Alicia has to say:

"This new project is not going so well. It is due this afternoon and I am not sure I covered all the angles. I really want it to be right. I focus best when things are predictable. A lot of things about this project have been anything but predictable. Sometimes my boss gets angry with me because I turn things in late. I take the heat. It's worth it.

"It's really important to make sure that everything is done properly. I need time to get it right. I have to make sure that people understand how hard I work and how much work I put into things.

"I will not hand in my work till I know that every part of it, every paragraph, and every number is perfect. What if someone says I made a mistake? I really wouldn't know how to handle it. What if they say I failed?"

Can you relate to Alicia?

Do you review and check, then double-check everything you do? Because you need perfection, do you have trouble making a decision? Do you care more about the project than the deadline? What do you do when you hand in something that is not perfect?

This little issue with perfection creates behaviors that can stop a company in its tracks. It spills over into family life, too. Have you ever met someone who alphabetizes their spice rack? Does that help or hinder their relationships with family?

The truth is that perfection is highly overrated. It is not achievable. Trying to be perfect can change the way you make decisions. After a point, you can't make a decision at all. Your choice might be wrong.

Perhaps you need more information. You might fail, so your solution is: don't make a decision. It's easier. It's safer. Why? Because you don't have to take a risk.

The Impact on Business however, can be huge. As a perfectionist, you could be missing deadlines and holding up projects. Ultimately, customers can become unhappy. You might even lose a few.

Perfectionism is a major problem for any organization. We have seen perfectionists become paralyzed, taking years and years on a project yet never being able to complete it.

Are you doing your best? Did you do everything you could within the time allotted?

How would you react if we said: "It's good enough"?

Can you accept it?

Can you embrace it?

Can you acknowledge that this is you?

Then, let it go.

Say these words out loud: "I am not a perfect person. I know that. I have to let it go and it's okay."

Being perfect is overrated. It's okay not to be perfect. We haven't met a perfect person yet. Be the person who is perfectly satisfied. Your life will change for the better.

Sherpa Inspiration: Laugh a Little

We worked with a sales manager. Ed had 25 years in the industry. He had great people skills.

Ed told us: "You know, 98% of the time I have no issues, no problems with people."

We asked: "What about the other 2%?" It stopped him in his tracks.

Ed admitted: "You know, sometimes things really don't go that well."

Ed is not perfect. Neither are we. Neither are you. With that in mind, you are on a journey. It's about you, how you behave, how you act, and what you say and do each day.

On this journey, you'll understand why certain people are the way they are, and how to live with that.

We'll share other peoples' lives and the things that they have taught us. We are not here to demean or belittle. We are here to put truth on your table.

We are doing it with a smile. Hopefully, you will laugh a little. You gotta laugh at life.

Look at all the behavior around you. A really great comedian is nothing more than an observer of other peoples' behavior. Keep your eyes open.

Most of all, take a breath. Don't be so hard on yourself. Smile! Laugh a little! We are here to share truth. We are here to shed light on behaviors you see every day. In the process, you can optimize your own.

Let's take a look at Christian.

Christian
Take the Money and Run

Christian is the CEO of an information technology company. They are out in Mountain View, California. Christian has moved past the startup phase. He now has 65 employees. Christian is all about work first, people second. He is not a bad guy. He is a hard worker, a man dedicated to his company. His people wish he could show the same kind of dedication to them.

People respect his skills. They'll tell you he's brilliant. They will also tell you Christian is absolutely indifferent when anyone talks about their family. He is not seen as concerned and caring. In fact, Christian will most likely turn you down if you ask for time off to go to a kid's recital or sporting event.

What would Christian say about himself?

"They do not understand at all. They are paid for what they do. Isn't a great paycheck enough? I pay them, which means I like them. Otherwise they wouldn't be here. So, what's the big deal? Why do people want me to stop what I'm doing and pat them on the back? What makes me saying something positive so important? I just don't get it.

"By the way, I am sick of people asking me: 'How was your weekend?' Come on! Nobody cares what I do, and I certainly don't care what they do."

Can you relate to Christian? Maybe you know him.

Do you have trouble taking time to appreciate your people?

How does that work at home with your kids and your spouse?

Recognition and respect are two of the most important motivators of all time. People love their work and stay at their job when they are recognized and respected. Recognition and respect are different things, but the behavior we are talking about covers both of these areas pretty well (or pretty poorly).

Are you all 'get it done,' all business, all work, and no play? If so, then you are taking your people for granted to some degree. You are treating them as objects. They feel as if they are nothing more than a paycheck.

What's the Impact on Business?

It's simple: people who don't feel recognized and respected will leave. You are playing the game like it's all about business but it's also about the people.

Be a complete, well rounded manager, or you'll never see the business results you want to see.

Here's the good news: Offering recognition and respect is not that difficult.

Recognition and respect can take many different forms. Maybe it's just two words: 'nice job.' It's up to you to hit the mark for your people. Who needs to be accepted, shown a little respect? Who needs a pat on the back once in a while? Who have you been ignoring?

Think of your kids. What if you never recognized them for good work or a well-played ball game? They would be miserable.

Recognition is a human need. It really feels good to be recognized.

The bottom line: the people who work for you need to be recognized. They need to be validated. Shouldn't your employees be happy working for you? Tell one person each day that they did a good job. Make it a habit. You'll be surprised. They'll be happier, and you will, too.

You might ask, what is the Impact on Business if you don't recognize your employees accomplishments?

You will have problems with morale and team work. Recognition is directly related to both of these.

The Impact on Business is turnover and poor morale.

That costs money.

Sherpa Inspiration: Behave Yourself

You went to school. You learned your ABC's, how to count, how to tie your shoes. You learned to study and get the right scores on your tests, the right letters on your report card. That went on for well over a decade. When you were done with school, you had knowledge. You had skills. You were ready to make money in the real world.

Skills:
Education in the professional, technical and business realm; that's what lands the job. That's what companies want.

Along the way, your teachers told you how to act, but that wasn't their main message. Your parents taught you manners and the importance of behaving and acting right, but it wasn't that deep. The bottom line is this: how to behave like a leader, and how to leverage self-awareness to better business behavior have been left to chance. Somehow, you are expected to figure them out for yourself.

Onward and upward. Fast forward a few more years. Based on education, training and experience, people have continuing success. People get promoted, move up the ranks. Not because of great behavior, but because of great skills.

Behavior:
With no leadership training or self-awareness, managers lead in the only way they know how. They 'shoot from the hip.' Why? They have spent all their time mastering the task, the project, and the skills. They know no other way.

What happens? Some people get beaten down. Empowerment goes out the window. There is no real accountability. Blame is in the air. No one owns anything. The list goes on and on. Ultimately, there is just too much damage. Someone has to give in or give up. Usually, it's the subordinate who does that. It's called employee turnover.

Unfortunately, this cycle does not stop there. An employee leaves, but they end up somewhere else with an equally bad boss. Inept leaders are everywhere, and everyone is suffering because of it. It's all a matter of behavior, something about which most people have never learned.

Here's a truth:

People are hired because of their skill and they are fired because of their behavior.

Here's one more:

People don't care how much you know . . .
until they know how much you care.

Robert
You Can Talk. Nobody's Listening

4

Robert is a sales manager for a food distributor in Detroit. It's a family business, and Robert seems to fit right in. He is a friendly, outgoing person. Robert enjoys bantering with his employees and his co-workers . . . to a fault.

This carries over to business meetings. People cannot get a word in edgewise when Robert talks. As soon as he opens his mouth, three things happen: People roll their eyes, check out, and get lost in the fascinating worlds of their iPhones.

This is how Robert describes himself:

"I love to talk. The things I have to say are so valuable. People know I am the expert in this organization. I know the customers and I know the products.

"I'm the 'go to' person when it comes to sharing my knowledge with others. When I get the floor, everyone will know what I think. I don't care how long it takes. I want to make sure everyone understands the situation and they don't miss out on a thing.

"It is important that there are no gaps. I know I won't allow any gaps. I will communicate as much as I have to so things aren't missed."

Without any doubt, you know someone who talks too much. People like Robert control entire conversations. They do not leave any room for input. They need to have the last word, no matter how long that might take.

Can you identify with Robert?

Have you ever wondered why people don't listen when you talk?

Here's the bottom line: People want to be heard. If you 'over talk,' they get tired of not being heard. They can't stand one-sided conversations. People are tired of not being asked for input. People give up. They haven't given up on you. They have given up on getting a few words in, because they have come to believe they will not be heard.

It wasn't always this way. Over time, however, they have come to know you. They want to be heard, but they have realized it's just not worth the effort.

So what do they do? Literally, they check out when you speak. They shut down. They pretend to pay attention with a nod of the head. They agree, even though they don't know what you just said.

Some go so far as leave the room or avoid you completely. The truth is, you probably have something incredibly valuable to say. But on the other hand, so do they.

What is the fundamental impact on business when:

➜ Someone always dominates conversations?

➜ A team does not have a leader?

➜ No one gets feedback?

➜ Not everyone is on the same page or in agreement?

How about establishing trust and participation within the team?

Unfortunately, we have seen this story play out too many times. Ultimately, the team leader has nobody left under him. In other cases, the only people left are the ones who are too scared to speak up or, by circumstance, cannot leave.

The individuals who need an environment of empowerment and inclusion end up seeking different opportunities at a different job.

It's time to allow others to have an opportunity in the 'speaking spotlight' as well. We know for a fact that there is not one person on the planet that doesn't want to be heard. You are no exception to the rule, but neither are they.

Believe it or not, there is a healthy balance between hearing and being heard. The key word is right there: balance. Not one sided conversations, but balance.

Where do you begin?

First and foremost, swallow the 'talk too much' pill if this is you.

Second, start by asking others what you can do to ensure that they are being heard.

These are two steps in the right direction.

Sherpa Inspiration: Do I Really Make An Impact?

We have done work with top executives at top companies. We heard it from the Sherpas of Nepal. People make an impact wherever they go. We work with people from across the country, and from all walks of life. Whether you are a front line worker at Coney Island amusement park or the CEO of a big company, your behavior has an Impact on Business.

Do you believe this?

Do you understand this?

We know it to be true.

On any given day, you can be the most important part of your business. At the end of the day, how important you are will come from treating others well.

Let's say you are a front line worker at Coney Island. Think about it:

Does it matter whether or not you reach out and communicate with customers?

What if you gossip with co-workers?

What if you share personal intimate details of your life?

If you do, how does that affect your work? Your relationships?

What is the Impact on Business when any of these things happen?

Imagine being CEO of a company with 5,000 employees:

What might happen if you don't stay in touch with people?

What if you don't communicate with the people around you?

What might happen if you don't attend all the meetings you are supposed to?

What happens if you don't tell your direct reports about an important decision?

What is the Impact on Business if any of these things happen?

Everything we choose to do and say makes a difference. From the entry level worker to the top level executive, negative behavior creates a negative Impact on Business. Positive behavior creates a positive Impact on Business.

The bottom line? Business has everything to do with people. People express themselves and make a difference through their behavior. Good or bad, behavior always has an Impact on Business.

This is an absolute truth.

Danielle
Let Me Hear Your Body Talk

Danielle is Deputy Commissioner of a government health care operation in Saint Paul, Minnesota. She has been with the agency for twenty years. Everyone knows, respects and trust Danielle. Their only grievance is that they just cannot understand her.

Her employees don't know whether she is happy or sad. Danielle's facial expression never changes (and we mean never). People have trouble fully engaging in conversations with Danielle. Sometimes, people say she is bored or disinterested. Along with her lack of facial expression, she always crosses her arms.

Here's how Danielle describes herself:

"People always read me incorrectly. I'm not intentionally ignoring or disagreeing with anyone.

"I know what I'm doing, but I'm not going to give it away. What I do NOT get called is pushover, stupid or doormat.

"I avoid eye contact when I am thinking.

"People say that I have a dead stare when they speak to me. Get over it folks, that's just me. Focus.

"I cross my arms when people are speaking to me. I am cold in my office and it helps me concentrate."

Can you identify with Danielle?

Do people misread you? Has anyone ever said, 'You are inconsiderate,' or 'You're not paying attention'? Do people take your non-verbal communication as personal attacks?

It's no secret. Your body language communicates just as powerfully as the words from your mouth. People can form opinions about what they see more quickly than they can process what they hear.

Are you sending the message you want to send when it comes to your body language?

Is your body language working for you?

Do people respond positively to your physical presence?

Do people enjoy being around you?

You might ask: what does body language have to do with Impact on Business?

More than you know. We have seen top executives shut down participation in their meetings, simply by having their arms crossed and a showing a stern face. If you are aloof, what kind of message does that send to your direct reports?

Here's your message: "I really don't have time to hear what you have to say. Do you know how busy I am?"

If you want to be viewed as an intimidating leader, this might work for you. However, if you follow that path you can forget about creating an environment that features trust and loyalty.

Embrace the fact you might be sending mixed messages via body language. Your 'gut check' is this:

➡ Watch your body language, watch your facial expressions. Are they saying what you want them to say?

➡ Are you delivering the message you want to send with your body language?

Here's a simple start:

Find three people you trust. Ask them candidly about the non-verbal message you send.

Ask them to describe your body language.

Ask them if they have ever misread you.

Be open to their answers.

Start the process of change by becoming very conscious of what your body is doing when you are talking.

It will take a while to make these changes, but it will have a huge Impact on Business.

Sherpa Inspiration: Other People

All of us care what others think about us. We base our self-image on what others think. There's no avoiding that. It's part of life. So what do people think?

➡ Do they like you?

➡ Do they think you are funny?

➡ Do they think you behave appropriately?

What about your boss?

➔ Does he say you do a good job?

➔ Does he like the way you follow through?

➔ Is he happy with the way you work with customers?

What people think about you is important. What you think about yourself is much more important.

Positive or negative, we all have an Impact on Business. Either way, it's up to you.

You are directly involved in creating your own IOB.

You are in complete control.

Nora
The Voice in My Head

Nora is the District Manager at a cosmetics plant. It's part of a huge company with headquarters in Paris. Nora works in New Jersey. These things happen. Nora knows the business well. She has been devoted to her job for 10 years.

People describe her as soft spoken, almost quiet. She is often overlooked in meetings. The best time to get Nora's opinion on something is to go to her office and sit down, one-on-one. Otherwise, you won't hear much from Nora.

Nora says this about herself:

"I disagree a lot with what people say in our business meetings, but I don't usually say anything. I certainly wouldn't disagree with anyone publicly. People probably think I don't have an opinion. But that's just not true. I'm actually a very smart and competent person. I didn't get to be district manager without knowing what I am doing.

"Some people just don't get me. If they just took a little extra time to ask what I think or just get my opinion, they'd really see what I'm made of . . . and what we should really be doing.

"When I am asked for an opinion I really need time to think it through and make sure it is a comprehensive, complete answer."

Can you identify with Nora?

Do you know someone who is never heard?

Someone who disappears in business meetings?

How about the person who always seems to agree with everything? You come to find out, weeks later, that the person actually disagreed, but never expressed an opinion.

Hear this loud and clear:

Quiet people may be too caught up in themselves. An effective business takes the time needed to get input from everyone, including you. That is a high standard, but it's true.

At the end of the day, everyone's responsibility is to ensure business success. People are the most critical element of this endeavor.

You are very important, but don't expect people to respect your opinion, or even know you have an opinion, if you are not sharing it.

So what is the Impact on Business when you don't speak up and make yourself heard in meetings?

What happens if specific roles and responsibilities are rolled out and you completely disagree with what you were assigned to do?

We've seen it happen too often, and the result is that you either disengage or disappear. You ignore an assignment or become invisible, all to the detriment of your team and your project.

If the project doesn't get done, customers complain and the Impact on Business is significant.

You have to work on your confidence. You are worthy of being heard.

You are an important member of the team.

You will NOT be heard unless you speak up and make a concerted effort toward active participation and input in your meetings.

Do you want your input valued?

Being valued is an important part of your achieving happiness.

You will be valued when you make yourself heard.

First step:

Identify your comfort zone. Figure out when you will speak out. What do the surroundings look like? Who is there? What is happening?

Next step:

Identify your panic zone. When do you fail to speak? When are you are afraid to step up and be heard?

Then:

Start expanding your comfort zone and re-defining your boundaries. Expand your comfort zone to include the people who need to hear you. How?

To be a confident person, you must act like a confident person.

Try it. You might just like it.

Sherpa Inspiration: This is Personal

Impact on Business is personal. It's what you do. Impact on Business is the difference you make.

It's your purpose and your meaning.

Finding a fresh, new self-awareness about what you do will make your life easier, more fulfilling and more enjoyable.

This takes work on your part. Coasting is not an option.

It is almost impossible to be personally fulfilled if you never work on being better.

Our friend Marshall Goldsmith sent a message in the title of his best-selling book, *What Got You Here . . . Won't Get You There.* What you have done so far has worked, to a certain extent.

To get better, the way you behave in the future has to get better. When you do the work, people do notice. Your cup will be filled.

Why do we focus on behavior? It's simple. People know you more for the way you act than they remember you for your accomplishments. The old adage, 'your works define you,' is not always true. What's more accurate is this adage, 'your actions define you.' Behavior. The way you act shows people who you are.

Want your life to be easier, more fulfilling and more enjoyable?

When you act well and behave well, you are respected. You are accepted. You are needed. You'll have great relationships.

You will be happier.

Duane
Can't We All Get Along?

Meet Duane. He's the director of marketing at a midsize clothing company in Hollywood, Florida. He really gets excited about Miami Beach International Fashion Week. Duane's employer makes clothes for the tourists, placed in boutique shops with high prices. He has thirty people reporting to him. It's a fast paced, dynamic environment.

Duane knows the business well. He has moved up through the ranks, having started in the mail room. Duane would tell you that he has quite a few personal friends working with him. Duane has never been able to fire a single person in all his years at this company. He will 're-gift' his difficult employees; moving them to other departments. It should be no surprise that conflict shuts Duane down.

Here's what he would say about himself:

"I really like being in my comfort zone. It is where I do my best thinking and my best work. I really don't want to confront people. At the end of the day, it's not worth it to me. I know exactly the right time to play the 'nice' card.

"Okay, so I don't like to deal with a difficult situation.

"What if they don't like me anymore?

"What if they think I am stupid?

"Confrontation is fighting . . . and fighting is bad. I have spent my life wanting to keep peace. Why should I start being mean and unkind?

"I have a good friend at work. I am sure she will do a great job in this position I am posting. It will be easy for me to hire her. That would be the easiest thing for me to do. I know she is not the best person for the job, but she is a good friend of mine. I know what she needs, she knows what I need.

"Sometimes, I know I have to meet face to face with someone. I think: 'This would be easier on the phone,' or 'I will e-mail them.' It's quicker and easier that way."

Can you identify with Duane?

What's the Impact on Business when people are 'too nice'?

What about avoiding confrontation?

In some cases, it can become as detrimental continually having to re-gift (send to another department) your friend to other parts of the organization because he is ineffective, but you cannot let him go. It might be working for you, but it's not working for anyone else.

The Impact on Business that comes from avoiding confrontation is huge. It is fundamentally a show stopper.

Your career could be held back because someone else avoids confrontation.

If this is you, you don't set expectations properly. You don't follow up on consequences, positive or negative. Expectations are not heard because people know you will not follow up or deal with things left undone. People walk on you because they know you will not deal with them or the situation.

Try it. Try the truth. Does your friend deserve the job? Is the confrontation necessary for effectiveness or continuous improvement? Is it truly because you are 'too nice'? Are you afraid of something?

Try the truth.

You may be very surprised at the outcome. The outcome is not what you are thinking it will be. Make all of these fears and doubts less of a big deal.

Confrontation is part of life. You have to do it to make things right.

Get comfortable with confrontation.

Be kind in your words, but deliver truth.

The truth is a 'must' in any situation. Stay truthful in your words and people will start hearing you.

The confrontation is never as bad as you think it will be. Understand: you are capable of dealing with anything.

Then, go ahead and try. Go slowly at first and reap the rewards of having people respect you, trust you and follow you.

Sherpa Inspiration: The Challenge

As experts in executive leadership, one of our critical roles is to ask challenging questions.

Unfortunately, most people don't think about that.

In fact most organizations avoid it. It's our role to 'go there,' no matter how uncomfortable it may be.

Why?

Because we know lives are at stake. We know people are getting hurt every day because of bad business behavior. We know if we don't do something about it, people will get hurt, and ultimately, the organizations they represent will get hurt.

We have to ask questions like:

What is the Impact on Business if you behave that way?

What will change, for better or worse, because of the way you are acting?

What Impact on Business are you creating with your behavior?

If your behavior really does affect the business, should you care?

Some food for thought:

Has anybody else's behavior had an impact on you, personally or professionally? Has someone else's behavior affected your happiness, your relationship, your attitude, the way you function day to day?

What if they took a moment to consider their behavior, their Impact on Business, and their impact on you?

If that's what you'd like from others, then what should you do yourself?

In all likelihood, nobody has challenged you in this way. Nobody has taught you these things. So, it all comes down to you. You will succeed to the degree you understand and create your personal Impact on Business.

Our Sherpa mantra is this:

When you are sick and tired of communicating, you still haven't communicated enough.

Plain and simple, talk it out.

Where Are They Now?

1 Sam was cold as ice, but he's warming up, and people are warming up to the idea of working for Sam.

2 In that Texas call center, Alicia has truly stopped trying to be perfect. Good enough is good enough. It wasn't as hard as she thought it would be.

3 Christian is President of a growing tech enterprise. He's learned to take a breath and enjoy his people. He started by going surfing with one of his techs, which they still do to this day.

4 Robert, that sales manager in Detroit? He still loves to talk, but he loves to listen, too. That's working for him. He has learned to count his sentences, and he always finishes with a question.

5 Danielle. Our Deputy Commissioner has learned to relax, unwrap her arms and legs, stretch out and welcome people. She started doing it as soon as she realized so many people were affected by it.

6 Nora was lost in New Jersey, but she's been found. Now, she speaks her mind at meetings, and she's managed to avert a couple of disasters in the last couple of months. She has been complimented so many times she has lost count.

7 Duane: It's not California, but it's still Hollywood. Our marketing manager can take on tough conversations a little better now, and he's hiring the right people, too. He's looking forward to Miami Beach International Fashion Week.

How about your story? It's yet to be written.

What have you learned from our seven stories?

Can you identify with any of these people?

What can you relate to?

What is your next step?

What's Your Impact on Business

You want to make a change. Here's exactly what to do:

➲ Acknowledge that your current behavior is clearly NOT working.

➲ Then observe: How and when it plays out.

Does this behavior occur with certain people?

At certain times?

It takes a while to identify the details. Don't be afraid to focus, observe and 'own it.'

➡ The third step is to figure out a replacement behavior. Probably the toughest step because you have to figure out "What might work better?" Ask someone close to you. Find a mentor. Don't be afraid to ask for help.

➡ The fourth and last step is to make sure this new behavior works. Evaluate it and see that the new behavior is better than the old behavior. Ask around. Do the people in your life recognize you have worked on it? Do they like this new behavior?

What's Your Impact on Business

Sherpa Inspiration: Community

When you see a change, keep us posted. Let us know about your happiness and success. There is a LinkedIn page devoted entirely to the readers of this book. Questions, concerns, thoughts, opinions, we are looking for them all.

www.linkedin.com/groups/impact-on-business-4420148

EPILOGUE

Behavior has no boundaries. This book is for everyone.

This book is for you.

In everything you do, in all that you are, is your behavior creating a positive or negative impact on you, on others, on your relationships, in your business, in your home, in your life?

Understand that behavior truly matters.

It impacts everything you do and everyone you come into contact with.

You want to change.

Where do you start?

You start understanding that if behaviors are not addressed, you ultimately will fail in the area of relationships and leadership.

You start with you.

Here's our challenge to you:

Get comfortable talking about behavior. Talk as comfortably about behavior with your people as you talk about their skills.

Imagine yourself being able to say something like this: "As much as your skills are important for this position, your behavior is just as important, so let's discuss them both. Let's list the skills needed for this job and list the behaviors we need, as well."

There's only one way this happens. Become as well-versed in behavior as you are in your skills, and that's through practice.

This is truth.

First, you have to practice on yourself. See how it works for you. Live it. Show it. Then, you can help your people work on their behavior.

What's Your Sugar?

A mother had come to her wit's end with her diabetic son. He would not stop eating sugar and she could not get him to stop.

Out of desperation, she sought out Mahatma Gandhi for help and asked that he tell her son to stop eating sugar.

Gandhi said to the mother: "Come back in three weeks."

Three weeks later, the mother and her son returned.

Gandhi looked at the son and said: "Stop eating sugar."

Baffled, the mother asked: "Why did you have me wait three weeks before you would say this?"

Gandhi replied: "Three weeks ago, I was still eating sugar."

What is your sugar?

Think about what Gandhi did, so he could deliver a message the mother and son could believe in. He had to stop eating sugar for himself before he would allow himself to help them.

We are saying 'Walk the walk.' Become a role model.

Start at home. How do you handle your teenage daughter coming home late? Once you understand that behavior truly has no boundaries, you will see that handling your daughter's tardiness is exactly the same thing as handling an employee who has missed a project deadline.

When you start looking at and addressing behaviors, you will see monumental changes. People will stay on the subject in meetings. They will care about each other a little more. People will speak up and offer valuable input to the situation at hand.

Can you imagine that change? Are you ready for the challenge? We know you are.

We started by talking about success and happiness.

Everyone in the world wants two things: to be happy and to be successful.

In order to accomplish both of these things, you have to understand your personal Impact on Business. Your IOB.

God be with you.

The Authors

Brenda Corbett
Author/Educator
Executive Coach

Rubi Ho
Author/Educator
Executive Coach

So, we have talked about you. Now, let's talk about us, your authors, the people sharing their thoughts with you.

Why should you listen to us?

What would qualify us to tell you how to act or what to do?

Actually, several things . . .

We are top-level executive coaches. It is no coincidence that we call our practice Sherpa Coaching. In many ways, the focus on business behavior parallels the Sherpa philosophy.

Executive coaching is all about business behavior. We are experts at changing behavior for the better.

We have developed a process for coaching that guarantees consistent results.

Our book about coaching is our textbook as we have taught and continue to teach at major universities, including The University of Georgia, Texas Christian University, and Miami of Ohio.

We coach and work with executive teams and leadership at major companies across the United States including a half-dozen 'household name' companies.

We have personally certified and directed hundreds of experts in their respective professions to become successful executive coaches.

As we train new coaches, we are privy to the details of thousands of coaching relationships. We know exactly what happens when behavior does change for the better and what it takes to get there.

We are your Sherpas.

Trust us as your guides.

We want nothing more than to see you at the top of your personal summit.